ELI ANDF

INNER
ENIGMA

Finding Peace in
Self-Discovery

Printed by:
Amazon Company

First Edition, 2024
ISBN 9-7988739682-5-1

INDEX

Introduction

I woke up abruptly in the middle of the night, and for a moment, everything seemed normal. The room was engulfed in darkness, only occasionally illuminated by the faint glimmer of a distant street lamp. The air, heavy and thick, clung to my lungs. But then, something shifted. A strange sense of oppression began to grow in my chest, as if the world were closing in on me, each beat of my heart echoing with a tinge of fear.

The silence turned into a deafening roar, and my skin suddenly turned cold and damp, as if the night had wrapped me in a chilling grip. Each breath became a challenge, as if oxygen had deserted the room, and I struggled to take in air.

My heart raced, galloping like untamed horses in my chest. It pounded so hard I could feel it in my throat, hammering against my temples. The room started spinning around me, as if it had been torn from reality and thrown into a chaotic whirlwind of bewildering emotions.

My mind filled with an indescribable fear, as if I had stumbled upon an abyss and found no ground beneath me. An uncontrollable sense overcame me that something terrible was about to happen, that my body was failing, that I was about to die.

My hands trembled, my muscles contorted in a disjointed dance, and my breathing became erratic, as if the air refused to fill my lungs. Thoughts, like a swarm of enraged bees, buzzed in my head, shouting that something was terribly wrong.

I tried to find a point of reference, a speck of calm amid the chaos, but every attempt was futile. Time seemed to distort, as if the clock had stopped and left me stranded in this whirlwind of terror and confusion.

I felt like I was crumbling from within, as if my emotional foundations were cracking. It was a storm of sensations, a symphony of fear and confusion wrapping me in its distressing embrace.

There was no escape. I was trapped in a body that seemed to betray me, in a mind entangled in its own thoughts. And amidst that chaos, I wished for one thing: to find a light, a ray of hope to pull me out of this dark abyss I found myself in.

Have you ever felt this way, overwhelmed by anxiety, disarmed by criticism, trapped in a state of persistent gloom, or questioned by a lack of self-confidence? Have you wondered where to find that spark of motivation when you need it most or struggled with the weight of self-forgiveness?

Life challenges us in ways that often catch us off guard, demanding answers for which we're not always prepared. These challenges, seemingly subtle but deeply rooted in our daily experiences, push us to seek understanding, strategies, and tools to effectively face them.

This book is a journey toward understanding and mastering these key areas of our existence. It's a compendium of lessons learned, personal reflections, and practical tools aimed at illuminating the often dark paths we all navigate at some point in our lives.

Within these pages, we'll explore anxiety and discover techniques to keep it at bay, approach criticism from a new perspective to turn it into opportunities for growth, unravel the knots of gloom, and learn to instill confidence in each step we take.

We'll discuss the importance of finding that spark of motivation that propels us forward and explore the depth of self-forgiveness, a powerful and liberating practice that allows us to embrace our past with compassion and move forward with determination.

Through stories, examples, and practical exercises, this book seeks not only to offer knowledge but also to be a companion guide on your journey toward a more fulfilling and balanced life. My hope is that you find here a refuge, a valuable resource, and a beacon of inspiration as you navigate the sometimes turbulent waters of human existence.

Together, we'll discover that we're not alone in these struggles and that often, the most powerful answers lie within ourselves. This is a book of self-discovery, growth, and, above all, compassion toward oneself.

I invite you to embark on this journey, to immerse yourself in these pages with an open mind and a willing heart, ready to embrace change and discover the greatness that lies within the journey toward self-realization.

Why are these lessons crucial?

In the whirlwind of modern life, we face challenges that often go unnoticed or underestimated. Anxiety can tint our social interactions, bad moods can darken our days, and criticisms can erode our self-confidence. These are just some of the obstacles we all encounter at different points in our lives, and learning to address them can be a transformative skill.

1. Managing Anxiety: Anxiety can be paralyzing, interfering with our emotional and physical well-being. Learning to manage it not only relieves stress but also helps us live a more fulfilling life in harmony with ourselves and others.
2. Dealing with Criticism: Criticisms, when not managed properly, can undermine our self-esteem and hinder our personal and professional growth. Learning to discern between constructive and destructive

criticisms can make the difference between stagnation and development.

3. Facing Bad Moods: Bad moods can influence our relationships, productivity, and ultimately, our happiness. Understanding how to address them can be key to regaining emotional balance and living more fully.

4. Developing Self-Confidence: Self-confidence is fundamental for facing challenges and pursuing goals. Learning to cultivate it is essential for personal growth and fulfillment.

5. Finding Motivation: Lack of motivation can hold us back on our path to achieving goals. Discovering how to stay motivated can make the difference between success and resignation.

6. Learning Self-Forgiveness: Self-forgiveness is a powerful tool to free ourselves from the weight of the past and move toward a fuller and more conscious life.

In summary, these lessons not only address individual aspects of our lives but also have a profound impact on our mental, emotional health, and interpersonal relationships. Mastering these skills not only improves our quality of life but also equips us with tools to face challenges with resilience and clarity. This book is meant to be a compass on your journey toward a more balanced and fulfilling life.

Personal Connection: My Journey Towards Understanding These Truths.

A few years ago, amidst a changing and challenging reality, I found myself on an emotional journey filled with unexpected twists. Anxiety became a constant companion, a shadow overshadowing my days and nights, fueled by the uncertainty of the pandemic and constant relocations that led me to change countries three times in less than two years.

As an immigrant, living outside my home country for such a long time has been both an emotional and practical journey. Adapting to new cultures and ways of life, language barriers, and nostalgia for the familiar have been challenges that tested my emotional resilience and adaptability.

In the midst of these tumultuous changes, I also went through a divorce, a painful transition that shook the foundations of what I considered my stable life.

Anxiety intensified, criticisms—both external and emerging from my own inner voice—eroded my confidence, and bad moods mingled with uncertainty, plunging me into an emotional storm.

It was in this maze of challenges and transitions that I began my inner search. I delved into books, deep conversations, and moments of personal reflection to find answers to the questions that arose amidst so many changes.

Each topic we'll explore in these pages isn't merely a theoretical concept but a truth lived and experienced firsthand. Anxiety, criticisms, bad moods, confidence, motivation, and self-forgiveness became focal points in my personal journey towards adaptation, healing, and growth.

This book is the result of that personal journey, a compilation of lessons learned during those challenging and revealing moments. I don't claim to be an infallible expert, but rather a fellow traveler sharing tools and perspectives that might illuminate your path, much like others have illuminated mine.

It's in personal experience, in the understanding and acceptance of these truths, where this book finds its foundation. My hope is that these pages serve as a beacon in your own storms, offering guidance and solace as you navigate the uncharted waters of life.

CHAPTER ONE

Anatomy of Anxiety

" Fear is the physical manifestation of mental weakness." - Mahatma Gandh

DEMYSTIFYING ANXIETY: WHAT IS IT AND HOW DOES IT AFFECT US?

Anxiety, a sensation many of us have experienced at some point in our lives, has been a companion not only to historical figures but also to ordinary individuals. Even brilliant minds like Charles Darwin grappled with their own internal demons. In his diary, Darwin described feeling 'old' due to his struggle with anxiety. Emily Dickinson, the famous poet, also captured in her verses the constant sensation of living on the edge, as if skiing on an emotional roller coaster.

However, anxiety makes no distinctions; no matter who you are or what your social status is, it can affect anyone. It's that constant stress, that chest-tightening worry that makes you feel like something bad is about to happen at any moment, even when you don't exactly know what it is. As someone who has gone through these ups and downs, I can say it's not an easy road.

Interestingly, science has also delved into this field. Studies, such as the one conducted by Kessler and his team (Kessler RC, 2005), have shown that anxiety is not just an emotional burden but also a physiological reality that alters our being. It has been evidenced that it affects our brain chemistry and has a significant impact on our body, not just our minds.

This journey toward understanding anxiety leads us to explore its anatomy, to unravel its complexities. We're not alone in this labyrinth; throughout history, brilliant minds and ordinary people alike have faced the same shadows. It's a journey toward acceptance and understanding, toward finding that exit leading us to the inner peace we so crave.

Anxiety is more than a mere feeling of worry or nervousness. It's a natural and adaptive response to stressful or unknown situations. However, when this response becomes overwhelming, persistent, or disproportionate to the actual situation, it can become a barrier to our mental health and well-being (López, M., 2019).

Dr. Maria López, a clinical psychologist, explains: 'Anxiety is the body's response to a perceived threat, whether physical, emotional, or psychological. It's an alarm signal that prepares us to deal with challenging situations' (López, M., 2019).

Scientific studies have revealed that anxiety can trigger a cascade of reactions in our body, from an increase in the release of stress hormones like cortisol and adrenaline to changes in brain activity affecting decision-making and risk perception (Smith, S., 2020).

Dr. Sarah Smith, in her research at Stanford University, discovered that chronic anxiety might be related to changes in the structure and function of the brain, particularly in areas involved in emotional regulation and decision-making (Smith, S., 2020).

Anxiety affects us in profound and varied ways. Have you ever felt that sensation of tightness in your chest, your heart racing, or your mind racing with unstoppable negative thoughts? These are some of the common symptoms of anxiety.

But it can also manifest itself in less evident ways: difficulty concentrating, sleep problems, irritability, or avoidance of certain situations.

I invite you to reflect: When have you experienced anxiety? How does it manifest in your body and mind? Has it affected your ability to perform certain activities or make decisions?

Although anxiety can be overwhelming, it's important to remember that there are effective strategies to manage it. From breathing techniques and meditation to cognitive-behavioral therapy and lifestyle changes, there's a variety of tools that can help reduce its impact on our lives (Brown, L., 2021).

In the following pages, we'll explore some of these strategies with the aim of providing practical tools to manage anxiety and regain control over your emotional well-being."

MANAGING ANXIETY IN EVERYDAY SITUATIONS.

Anxiety can show up as an unwelcome guest at the most inconvenient times, but developing a set of practical tools can help you navigate it with grace and resilience in your day-to-day life.

Conscious Breathing: Deep breathing is a direct gateway to calmness. Imagine your breath as waves: inhale as you count to five, allowing the air to fill your body, then exhale slowly counting to eight, releasing any built-up tension. Repeat this exercise, letting each breath bring peace and stillness to your mind.

Mindfulness Exploration: Practicing mindfulness is like strolling through a serene garden. Dedicate a few minutes each day to tune into your senses: observe the sounds around you, feel the texture of things, acknowledge the scents that come your way. This connection to the present can divert your mind from future worries and past burdens, creating space for tranquility.

Endorphin Dance: Why not turn physical activity into a dance? Whether it's an energetic walk, a yoga session, or a dance class: exercise releases endorphins, those natural chemicals that uplift mood and reduce anxiety. Dance to the rhythm of your heart and feel the tension dissolve with each movement.

Self-Care Sanctuary: Allocate time for a personal sanctuary. Find that place, whether it's a cozy corner at home or an outdoor spot, where you can engage in restorative activities. Allow yourself to enjoy a cup of aromatic tea, immerse in a relaxing bath, or simply sit in silence, embracing the peace that comes with self-care.

Support Network and Dialogue: Building bridges with others is building an emotional safety net. Share your concerns with close friends or family, or consider talking to a professional. Expressing what you feel can lighten the load and provide valuable perspectives.

These strategies not only offer practical ways to manage anxiety but also invite a more creative and sensory approach to address it. Experiment with these tools and discover how each can become your ally on the journey toward calmness and emotional resilience in everyday life.

CHAPTER TWO

Sailing Through the
Tides of Criticism

" Criticism is something you can easily avoid by saying nothing, doing nothing, and being nothing. " - Aristotle

THE IMPACT OF CRITICISM ON OUR SELF-ESTEEM.

Criticism, those things that sometimes hit you like a storm, don't discriminate against anyone, not even top athletes. Remember Michael Jordan's quote: 'I've failed over and over and over again in my life. That's why I've succeeded.' That says a lot, doesn't it? It's like telling us that mistakes and criticism are part of the path to success.

But criticism doesn't just target the most famous, you know? We all encounter those opinions that dent our self-esteem. And believe me, I know how it feels. Science has delved into this too. A study by Harwood and Swain (Harwood, C. G., & Swain, A. B., 2001) shows that criticism can make you doubt yourself and affect your performance in sports. So, handling those opinions well seems to be key to maintaining your level.

In this journey through the tides of criticism, we learn that, although they hurt, those opinions don't define our worth or what we're capable of achieving. It's like realizing that criticisms are like waves in the sea: they come and go, but they don't sink you if you know how to ride them.

Criticism can be a double-edged sword: on one hand, it can offer opportunities for growth and improvement, but on the other, it can inflict significant damage to our self-esteem. The impact of criticism on our perception of ourselves can be profound and lasting.

In simple terms, criticism can pierce the deepest layers of our self-confidence. When constructive, it can offer valuable external perspective, providing an opportunity to learn and grow. However, destructive or ill-intentioned criticism can gradually erode our confidence and self-esteem.

Hurtful words can resonate in the depths of our identity, sowing seeds of doubt and questioning. Constant criticism can create negative self-talk, feeding a narrative that tells us we're not good enough, smart enough, or capable enough. This can lead to decreased self-esteem and the development of deep-seated insecurities.

Criticism can have an even more potent impact when it comes from significant sources in our lives, such as close friends, family, or authority figures. The opinions of these people can carry stronger emotional weight, thus having a deeper impact on our self-esteem.

For many, negative criticism can be difficult to shake off. They linger in our minds, reverberate in our actions, and affect our self-perception in various situations. Often, we internalize these criticisms, turning them into truths that define ourselves, even when they're merely others' opinions.

However, it's crucial to remember that our worth isn't determined by others' opinions. Learning to separate our identity from external criticism and cultivating a solid self-esteem are crucial processes in resilience against damaging criticism.

In the next chapter, we'll explore strategies to handle and filter criticism, how to discern between constructive and destructive criticism, and how to protect our self-esteem while using criticism for personal growth.

STRATEGIES TO TRANSFORM DESTRUCTIVE CRITICISM INTO GROWTH OPPORTUNITIES.

"Transforming destructive criticism into growth opportunities is a challenging yet crucial process to bolster our emotional resilience. Here are some strategies to do so:

1. Emotionally detach from the criticism: Try to distance yourself emotionally from the initial criticism. Acknowledge your emotions but don't let them overpower your response. Take deep breaths and take a moment to objectively analyze the criticism.

2. Identify the underlying intention: Try to understand the motivation behind the criticism. Sometimes, people express criticism with good intentions, even if their communication might be inappropriate. Look for the underlying message beyond the words.
3. information filtering: Learn to discern between constructive and destructive criticism. Constructive criticism offers specific advice for improvement, while destructive criticism might be personal attacks or vague. Focus on criticisms that provide clear growth opportunities.
4. Ask and clarify: If the criticism isn't clear, consider asking the critic for additional details. Sometimes, through open communication, you can better understand the other person's perspective and find real areas for improvement.
5. Focus on learning: Shift the mindset from viewing criticism as personal attacks to seeing them as opportunities to learn and grow. Reinforce the idea that personal development involves recognizing areas for improvement.
6. Extract lessons and set goals: Identify valid points within the criticism and use those aspects to set growth goals. Turn criticism into

a springboard for personal and professional development.

7. Nurture self-esteem: Maintain a healthy and strong self-esteem. Acknowledge your strengths and achievements, remembering that criticisms don't define your worth as a person.

8. Seek support: Talk to friends, family, or a trusted mentor for additional perspectives. External support can help you process criticisms and find effective ways to grow.

By implementing these strategies, you can transform the negative impact of destructive criticism into opportunities for improvement and development. Remember, the goal isn't to completely eliminate negative criticism but to learn to handle it constructively to foster your personal and professional growth.

CHAPTER THREE

Toward Understanding Bad Moods

" Bad mood is a passing cloud that can disperse with the light of reflection and the power of self-control. "

Unearthing the Roots of Bad Moods and Their Impact on Our Lives.

Have you ever seen "Falling Down"? It's like a chronicle of that moment when you feel at the limit, like Michael Douglas in the movie, you know? He just explodes with all those things that frustrate him. It's like life turns against you and everything gets complicated.

But hey, bad mood isn't just a movie thing. We've all had those dark days where it seems like everything conspires to annoy you. I've been there, I understand how challenging it can be to keep calm when everything seems to go wrong.

The movie shows us something important: sometimes, bad mood is like a thermometer for all those pressures and tensions we carry. It can be like that pressure cooker that finally blows up, doesn't it?

In this journey to understand bad mood, we realize that even in movies, we see that struggle against these emotional states. Accepting that bad mood is part of life helps us understand ourselves better, connect with our emotions, and seek our inner peace. So, how about we learn to ride those waves of bad mood instead of letting them drag us down?

Bad mood can be like a sudden storm that clouds our thoughts and darkens our mood. Discovering its roots and understanding its impact on our lives is crucial to find effective ways to manage it.

The roots of bad mood can be diverse and often lie in our past experiences, accumulated stress, lack of sleep, emotional health, or even biological factors. Sometimes, a specific situation can trigger bad mood, while at other times, it may result from a buildup of internal tensions.

Bad mood can dramatically affect our interactions with others and our ability to function optimally in our daily responsibilities. It can manifest as irritability, impatience, lack of concentration, or even more negative behaviors.

Chronic stress, persistent worries, or unresolved issues can feed bad mood, making it a constant companion in our lives. Furthermore, the impact of bad mood can extend beyond our own experience, affecting our personal relationships, work environments, or even how we perceive ourselves.

When we're in a bad mood, our social interactions can be affected. We might be less understanding, less tolerant, or even more prone to expressing negativity towards others. This can create a cycle that perpetuates bad mood, affecting not only our well-being but also those around us.

Understanding the roots of bad mood and its impact gives us the opportunity to address it more effectively. Identifying the underlying causes, seeking ways to manage stress, cultivating empathy towards ourselves and others, as well as practicing self-reflection, are important steps to illuminate and dissipate the cloud of bad mood in our lives.

SIMPLE EXERCISES AND PRACTICES TO CHANGE YOUR MOOD AND CULTIVATE JOY.

"Cultivating joy and changing our mood can be a challenge, but there are simple practices and exercises that can be effective in promoting a positive change:

Gratitude Practice: Keeping a gratitude journal can be transformative. Every day, write down three things you are grateful for. This can help shift your focus from the negative to the positive, cultivating a more optimistic mindset.

Regular Physical Exercise: Exercise releases endorphins, brain chemicals that act as natural painkillers and improve mood. Engaging in physical activities you enjoy, such as walking, dancing, or practicing yoga, can uplift your spirits.

Meditation and Mindfulness: Dedicate a few minutes each day to meditate or practice mindfulness. Focus on your breath, observe your thoughts without judgment, and stay present in the current moment. This can help calm the mind and reduce stress, allowing joy to emerge.

Social Connection: Spending time with friends, family, or people who provide support can increase your happiness. Human connection and emotional support can be powerful drivers of a positive mood.

Time for Pleasurable Activities: Set aside daily time for activities you truly enjoy. It could be reading, painting, listening to music, cooking, or any hobby that makes you feel good. These activities can lift your spirits and increase your sense of well-being.

Laughter and Humor: Laugh as much as you can. Watching a funny movie, listening to a comedy monologue, or simply laughing with friends can significantly boost your mood.

Self-Care: Practicing self-care is vital. Take a relaxing bath, prepare a special meal for yourself, go for a nature walk, or simply dedicate time to rest and relax.

Positive Visualization: Take a few minutes to visualize a moment, place, or situation that brings you joy. Immerse yourself in the positive details and sensations that this image brings.

These exercises and practices are simple yet effective in changing mood and cultivating joy in daily life. Gradually incorporating these habits can contribute to a positive change in your emotional well-being and greater overall happiness.

CHAPTER FOUR

Fostering Inner Confidence

" Inner confidence is the foundation upon which we build our personal success and happiness. "

THE IMPORTANCE OF CONFIDENCE IN PERSONAL GROWTH.

Inner confidence, that glow that makes you shine from within, can be like the best-kept secret of some people. It's like that spark that illuminates everything you do. Think of people like Oprah Winfrey, you know? She once said, "Confidence is what allows you to stand up and speak. That's what I want for everyone."

But of course, confidence isn't something that just appears out of nowhere. All of us, at some point, have had to cultivate it like a seed that grows slowly. As someone who has gone through those moments of doubt, I understand how important that self-confidence is.

Inner confidence is like that muscle that strengthens over time. It's not just about believing in yourself; it's knowing that even if you stumble, you have the strength to rise.

In this journey to cultivate inner confidence, we realize that even the most secure people have gone through moments of insecurity. Accepting that confidence is a path of learning helps us grow and be more understanding of ourselves and others. What if we aim to nurture that inner confidence and let it shine more every day?

Self-confidence is a fundamental ingredient in the journey towards personal growth. Its importance lies in various aspects that directly impact our development and well-being:

I. Exploration and self-discovery: Confidence acts as a guiding light in exploring our capabilities, interests, and values. When we trust ourselves, we feel more motivated to explore new horizons, try new things, and discover unexplored aspects of our personality. This fuels an ongoing process of self-awareness and self-discovery.

2. Facing challenges: Self-confidence acts as a cushion against adversity. It gives us the necessary strength to face challenges and overcome obstacles. The assurance in our abilities helps us stay calm and determined even in tough times, enabling us to seek creative solutions and adapt to circumstances.

3. Growth and learning: Confidence is a key facilitator of continuous learning. When we trust our ability to learn and grow, we become more receptive to new ideas, experiences, and knowledge. We are more willing to take on intellectual challenges and develop skills that contribute to our personal and professional growth.

4. Decision-making: Self-confidence plays a crucial role in decision-making. Solid self-confidence allows us to better assess situations, trust our choices, and make informed decisions. This empowers us to take responsibility for our lives and chart our own course.

5. Interpersonal relationships: Self-confidence influences how we relate to others. Healthy self-confidence allows us to build stronger relationships based on authenticity and mutual respect. Additionally, it makes us more resilient to negative opinions from others, enabling us

to maintain healthier and more meaningful relationships.

6. Emotional well-being: Self-confidence is closely related to emotional well-being. People with positive self-confidence tend to experience less anxiety, stress, and depression. They feel more capable of facing emotional challenges and are more resilient in the face of life's difficulties.

In summary, self-confidence is a fundamental pillar in personal growth. It strengthens our ability to explore, face challenges, learn, make assertive decisions, and build healthy relationships, all of which significantly contribute to our overall well-being and holistic development.

Practical Steps to Build and Maintain Self-Confidence.

Self-confidence is like a seed that, when cared for and nurtured, grows and strengthens our entire being. Building and maintaining this self-confidence is a gradual process that requires consistent attention and practice. Now, we'll explore practical steps to cultivate and sustain solid self-confidence.

Self-awareness: The Root of Confidence. Before building your confidence, you need to know yourself. Examine your strengths, skills, and past accomplishments. Make a list of your successes, no matter how small. This acknowledgment will give you a solid foundation to build your confidence upon.

Realistic Goals, Concrete Steps. Set achievable goals. Start with small objectives and gradually increase their complexity. Celebrating each achievement reinforces your confidence in your ability to accomplish bigger things.

Learning from Mistakes: The Power of Resilience. Mistakes are disguised lessons. Instead of fearing them, accept them as part of the learning process. Reflect on them and make adjustments for the future. The ability to learn and grow through experience enhances your self-confidence.

Develop Your Skills: The Path to Empowerment. Continuously seek knowledge and acquire skills. Constant learning and improvement increase your confidence in your ability to face new challenges and situations.

Face Your Fears: Overcoming Barriers. Confront your fears gradually. Taking steps outside your comfort zone allows you to gain confidence in your ability to overcome obstacles and challenges.

Mind Your Self-Talk: Empowering Words. Your internal voice has a significant impact on your self-confidence. Replace negative thoughts with positive and realistic affirmations. Speaking to yourself kindly and compassionately strengthens your confidence.

The Power of Self-Care: Well-being that Drives Confidence Self-care is key. Proper sleep, healthy eating, and exercise significantly contribute to your emotional well-being, providing a solid foundation for your confidence.

In summary, self-confidence is an evolving process. By following these practical steps and committing to your personal growth, you'll be laying the groundwork for lasting confidence and a solid self-esteem.

CHAPTER FIVE

Igniting the Spark
of Motivation

" Motivation is the spark that ignites action, turning dreams into achievements and possibilities into realities. "

THE INVISIBLE ENGINE: INTRINSIC AND EXTRINSIC MOTIVATION.

Do you know Tony Robbins? That guy is like the guru of motivation, you know? He has this quote that goes, 'Successful people do what unsuccessful people are not willing to do. They don't wish to do it, they don't like to do it, it's not convenient to do it.' It's a reminder that the key is taking action even when it's not easy.

But hey, finding that motivational spark isn't always a walk in the park. We've all had those days when it feels like the energy just isn't there. I've been through that, I know how challenging it can be to keep that flame burning.

Motivation is like a rechargeable battery. Sometimes it's full, and other times it feels like it's running low. It's not just about feeling like it, it's about finding that strength and dedication to keep going even when things get tough.

In this journey to ignite that spark of motivation, we understand that even the most successful people have had moments of doubt. Knowing that finding motivation can be a process helps us take a breather and look for different ways to stay focused and motivated. So, how can we take charge and maintain that motivation on tough days?

Motivation drives our actions and determines our persistence in achieving goals. In this chapter, we'll explore two facets of motivation: intrinsic, rooted in our personal interests and values, and extrinsic, influenced by external factors.

Intrinsic Motivation: Nurturing the Inner Fire

Intrinsic motivation arises from the depths of our being. It's linked to personal interests, values, and passions. Exploring what excites and brings us joy is key to nurturing this form of motivation. Personal satisfaction and enjoyment of the activity itself are its main drivers.

Extrinsic Motivation: The Influence of the Environment

Extrinsic motivation stems from external rewards like recognition, money, or prizes. Often, it's linked to specific goals or tangible incentives. While it can drive short-term performance, its influence may be less enduring than intrinsic motivation.

Dynamic Between Both Forms of Motivation

The two forms of motivation aren't exclusive; they often coexist and complement each other. In many scenarios, intrinsic motivation can fuel and enhance extrinsic motivation. Understanding how they intertwine and how they can mutually bolster each other is crucial for maintaining effective balance.

Cultivating Intrinsic Motivation

Exploring our interests, setting meaningful personal goals, and finding purpose in our daily activities are ways to nurture intrinsic motivation. This form of motivation strengthens when we emotionally connect with what we do.

Balancing Extrinsic Motivation

Leveraging external incentives can be helpful, but it's important not to rely solely on them. Finding alignment between external goals and our personal values is essential to using extrinsic motivation effectively and sustainably.

Empowering Motivation: Key to Success

Understanding the complexity of both forms of motivation and learning to cultivate them in harmony is essential for maintaining a steady momentum towards success. Recognizing how they intertwine and how they can mutually propel each other is crucial to achieving goals meaningfully and sustainably.

By exploring and understanding intrinsic and extrinsic motivation, we can use both as powerful tools on our journey towards goal achievement and personal fulfillment.

Effective Strategies to Find and Nurture Motivation in Daily Life.

Motivation is like a fire that requires constant care to stay ignited. Here, we explore practical strategies to find and nurture motivation in your daily life.

Set Clear and Meaningful Goals

Defining specific and achievable goals provides direction and a clear purpose. Break your objectives into smaller, manageable steps to ease your progress and keep you focused.

Find Your Why

Connect your daily activities with a deeper purpose. Discover why it's important for you to accomplish certain tasks. Understanding the meaning behind your actions boosts your intrinsic motivation.

Create a Motivation-Friendly Environment

Establish an environment that fuels your goals. Organize your workspace to eliminate distractions and encourage focus. A tidy and welcoming environment can enhance your willingness to work towards your goals.

Role Models and Inspiration

Seek role models or inspiration from individuals who have achieved what you desire. Learn from their experiences and use their success as motivation to move forward in your own pursuits.

Self-Care and Compassion

Self-care is essential. Practice self-compassion, acknowledging that progress isn't always linear. Grant yourself permission to make mistakes and learn from them. Additionally, tend to your physical and mental well-being.

Visualization and Constant Reminders

Regularly visualize your goals and objectives. Use visual reminders like sticky notes or images to keep alive the vision of what you aim to achieve.

Celebrate Your Achievements

Acknowledge and celebrate every achievement, no matter how small. Celebrating your progress reinforces the sense of accomplishment and propels you forward.

Flexibility and Adaptability

Be flexible and adaptable in your approach. Sometimes, plans can change, and being open to adjustments allows you to maintain momentum even in the face of unexpected challenges.

These strategies can help you find and nurture motivation in your day-to-day, equipping you with tools to keep the flame alive that drives your progress towards your goals and dreams."

CHAPTER SIX

The Art of
Self-Forgiveness

" *Personal forgiveness is the freedom you grant your soul to heal, let go, and flourish in new beginnings.* "

THE ROLE OF SELF-FORGIVENESS IN HEALING AND PERSONAL GROWTH.

"The person hardest to forgive is the one I still have to face: myself." This poignant phrase by Edith Eva Eger, narrated in her book "The Choice: Embrace the Possible," opens the door to a deep and universal truth about self-forgiveness.

Edith Eva Eger, a Holocaust survivor, carried an overwhelming burden: the feeling of guilt for having survived while her mother did not. This emotional weight stayed with her for a long time, leading her to face the difficult task of forgiving herself for a situation that was entirely out of her control.

This powerful testimony prompts us to reflect on self-forgiveness as an internal struggle, where the person we find most difficult to forgive is often ourselves. Guilt, remorse, and self-compassion are emotions that can entangle us in a labyrinth of pain.

The journey toward self-forgiveness is a process of understanding and acceptance. It's not about justifying circumstances but freeing ourselves from the emotional burden that keeps us tethered to the past. Edith Eva Eger shows us that self-forgiveness is an act of compassion toward oneself, a recognition that even in the most heartbreaking situations, we deserve understanding and healing.

Eger's message highlights the importance of letting go of self-judgment and finding inner peace. Accepting our own limitations, understanding that we cannot change the past, and forgiving ourselves are vital steps toward emotional healing and building a more compassionate and hopeful future.

Self-forgiveness is an act of self-compassion, a powerful tool that facilitates emotional healing and personal growth. Next, we'll explore the fundamental role self-forgiveness plays in our inner evolution.

Understanding Self-Forgiveness

Self-forgiveness involves freeing ourselves from guilt, remorse, and self-criticism. It's a process of accepting and compassionately understanding our own actions and past experiences.

Healing Through Forgiveness

Self-forgiveness is a path toward emotional healing. By releasing the negative emotional burden, we allow internal wounds to heal and initiate a process of inner renewal.

Growth and Transformation

Forgiving ourselves is an act of self-love that fosters personal growth. It enables us to learn from our mistakes, develop resilience, and move toward a stronger and more compassionate version of ourselves.

Self-Compassion and Authenticity

Self-forgiveness is intrinsically linked to self-compassion. Recognizing our humanity and accepting our imperfections allows us to live authentically and kindly toward ourselves.

Release and New Beginnings

By forgiving ourselves, we open the door to new beginnings. We free ourselves from the weight of the past, allowing us to move forward with a renewed mindset and the ability to embrace the present with serenity.

Tools for Self-Forgiveness

We'll explore practical strategies for cultivating self-forgiveness. From practicing self-compassion to guided reflection, these tools will help us progress toward internal reconciliation.

Journey Toward Inner Peace

Self-forgiveness is an ongoing journey. Through reflection, acceptance, and consistent practice of self-compassion, we embark on a path toward inner peace and personal fulfillment.

Self-forgiveness is a liberating process that enables internal transformation and opens doors to a more fulfilling future. Understanding its significance and practicing its art guides us toward a fuller and more authentic life.

EXERCISES AND REFLECTIONS TO PRACTICE SELF-CARE AND SELF-COMPASSION.

Self-care and self-compassion are fundamental elements to maintain a balanced mental and emotional health in our daily lives. Cultivating these practices can strengthen our ability to face challenges, manage stress, and improve our relationship with ourselves. Here, we'll explore a series of exercises and reflections designed to nurture self-care and foster self-compassion.

1. Conscious Breathing and Mindfulness. Take a few minutes each day to practice conscious breathing. Sit comfortably, close your eyes, and focus on your breath. Observe how the air enters and leaves your body. This

helps calm the mind and be present in the current moment.

2. Self-Compassion Visualization. Imagine a safe and tranquil place. Visualize yourself in this environment, surrounded by love and understanding. Emotionally connect with yourself, sending kind and supportive words.

3. Self-Compassion Letter. Write a letter to yourself from a place of compassion and understanding. Acknowledge your struggles and challenges without judgment. Express yourself kindly, offering comfort and encouragement.

4. Conscious Emotion Reflection. Take time to reflect on your daily emotions. Identify how you feel without judging those emotions. Recognize that all emotions are valid and normal.

5. Gratitude Practices and Positive Affirmations. Create a daily ritual to express gratitude. List things you are thankful for. Additionally, practice positive affirmations that reinforce your self-esteem and self-love.

6. Managing Self-Criticism. Observe your self-critical thoughts with curiosity and compassion. Replace these thoughts with

kinder and more realistic affirmations. Allow yourself to make mistakes and learn from them. 7. Self-Compassion in Challenging Moments. When facing challenges or difficult moments, remember to be kind to yourself. Use conscious breathing or visualization to calm yourself. Accept your emotions and look for ways to console yourself.

These exercises and reflections can be integrated into your daily routine to foster a healthier relationship with yourself. By practicing self-care and self-compassion, you cultivate the ability to emotionally care for yourself and create an internal space of acceptance and love. Integrating these practices into your life can promote lasting well-being and a more compassionate relationship with yourself.

I've provided a series of practical tools to integrate self-care and self-compassion into daily life, thereby strengthening mental and emotional health.

Conclusions

Recap of key lessons and practical advice.

Throughout this journey of exploring self-care, self-compassion, and personal growth, we've delved into valuable lessons that can strengthen our connection with ourselves and enhance our quality of life. Below, we recap key lessons and offer practical advice to integrate these learnings into our daily routine.

I. Self-Care as a Priority: Self-care is not a luxury but a necessity. Prioritizing time to tend to our physical, emotional, and mental needs is essential for maintaining a healthy balance in everyday life.

2. Mindfulness and Conscious Breathing Practices: Regular mindfulness practice and conscious breathing can calm the mind, reduce stress, and enhance our ability to be present in the current moment.

3. Cultivating Self-Compassion: Self-compassion involves treating ourselves with the same kindness and compassion we would offer to a friend in times of difficulty. Embracing our imperfections and being understanding toward ourselves fosters a more loving and compassionate internal environment.
4. Forgiveness and Personal Growth: Personal forgiveness is liberating. Learning to forgive ourselves enables us to let go of the weight of the past and move toward significant personal growth.
5. Self-Reflection Practices: Dedicate time to reflect on our emotions, thoughts, and behavioral patterns for a better understanding of ourselves. These reflections help identify areas for improvement and personal growth.

Practical Tips:

Establish Self-Care Routines: Incorporate self-care activities into your daily life, whether they're small or significant.

Practice Gratitude: Maintain a gratitude journal to focus on the positive aspects of life.

Seek Support: Don't hesitate to seek professional help or support from friends and family when needed.

Embrace Vulnerability: Recognize and accept your vulnerabilities as part of your humanity.

Be Kind to Yourself: Speak to yourself with kindness and understanding at all times.

Integrating these lessons and practical tips into your daily life can significantly contribute to your emotional and mental well-being. By prioritizing self-care, cultivating self-compassion, and practicing self-reflection, you can nurture a more loving and compassionate relationship with yourself, thereby promoting continuous personal growth and a fuller life.

We've summarized key lessons and provided practical advice for implementation, offering a useful guide for those seeking to improve their emotional and mental well-being.

Additional resources to further delve into each topic.

The pursuit of emotional well-being and personal growth is an ongoing and enriching journey. If you wish to delve deeper into the topics we've explored thus far, there's a variety of resources available that can offer even more insights and practical tools. Below are additional resources to continue nurturing self-care, self-compassion, and personal growth:

Books on Self-Care and Well-being:

"The Power of Now" by Eckhart Tolle: Explores the significance of mindfulness and living in the present moment.

"The Art of Loving" by Erich Fromm: Offers perspectives on love and compassion, including the relationship with oneself.

"Self-Compassion: The Proven Power of Being Kind to Yourself" by Kristin Neff: Delves into the practice of self-compassion and provides practical exercises.

Meditation and Mindfulness Resources:

Meditation Apps: Calm, Headspace, and Insight Timer offer a variety of guided meditations and mindfulness exercises.

Videos and Podcasts: Platforms like YouTube and podcasts dedicated to mindfulness and meditation offer a wide range of free resources.

Online Courses and Workshops: Coursera and Udemy offer courses on mindfulness, self-compassion, stress management, and personal growth.

Coaching Platforms: Look for coaching professionals offering workshops or individual sessions on self-discovery and personal growth.

Professional Support and Support Communities:

Therapy and Counseling: Consulting a therapist or counselor can be beneficial for addressing specific issues and receiving personalized support.

Support Groups: Engaging in online or in-person support groups connects you with individuals sharing similar experiences and provides a supportive environment.

Social Media and Blog Resources:

Following Experts: Seek profiles of experts in self-care, positive psychology, mindfulness, and self-compassion on social media platforms like Instagram and Twitter.

Blogs and Websites: Many blogs and websites offer quality content on topics related to emotional well-being and personal development.

These additional resources provide opportunities to continue learning and growing on your journey toward self-care, self-compassion, and personal growth. Exploring these sources can offer new perspectives, practical tools, and ongoing support in your pursuit of well-being and personal development.

This diverse list of resources is for those interested in continuing their exploration of self-care, self-compassion, and personal growth, providing a useful guide for advancing further on their journey of emotional and mental well-being.

Epilogue

A Journey Towards Inner Fulfillment.

"In our journey of exploration into self-care, self-compassion, and personal growth, we've navigated through the complexities of our relationship with ourselves. We've discovered that tending to our mental, emotional, and spiritual well-being is foundational to a fulfilling and satisfying life.

By learning to prioritize ourselves, practicing self-compassion, and forgiving ourselves, we've sown seeds of love and acceptance in the garden of our being. We've recognized beauty in our imperfections and strength in our vulnerabilities.

This journey isn't a final destination but an ongoing process of self-discovery and growth. Each day offers new opportunities to practice self-care, nurture self-compassion, and progress on our path toward inner fulfillment.

Remember, self-care isn't selfishness; it's an act of love towards ourselves that empowers us to be more compassionate and generous towards others. Self-compassion isn't weakness; it's the source of our inner strength and our ability to face challenges with grace and understanding.

In this journey, always remember:

Be kind to yourself: Speak to yourself with kindness and understanding at all times.

Prioritize your well-being: Caring for your mental and emotional health is crucial for a fulfilling life.

Embrace your humanity: Acknowledge and accept your imperfections as part of your unique beauty.

May this journey toward inner fulfillment be a continuous evolution, a path filled with learning, self-love, and acceptance. May each step bring us closer to internal harmony and a deeper connection with ourselves and others.

In the realm of self-care and self-compassion, we find the key to unlocking a fuller and more meaningful life. May this journey inspire us to keep exploring, growing, and celebrating the beauty of our being at every step along the way.

Acknowledgments

As I pen down these words, I feel an overwhelming need to express my deepest gratitude. In moments when the world seemed to crumble around me, you've been my anchor, my light, and my strength.

To each of you who stood by me during my toughest times, I want to convey that your support has been invaluable. Your understanding, patience, and unconditional love have been like a balm to my soul when I needed it most.

To my family, who have been my rock, my safe haven amid the storm, I lack adequate words to express my gratitude.

To my friends, my partners in laughter and confidants in moments of tears, thank you for standing by me regardless of distance or circumstances. Your empathetic listening and honest advice have been an invaluable gift in my life.

About the Author

Eli Andrade is a Brazilian writer and theologian who has relocated several times around the world in search of new adventures and experiences. After spending over 15 years in Spain and more than 2 years in England, Eli has gained a global perspective and a profound understanding of the challenges and concerns people face today.

He's an enthusiast of Jeffrey Archer's novels and loves debating diverse topics, from politics to religion, art, and technology. But his true passion lies in aiding people through literature. Currently, he is working on various projects related to mental, social, and spiritual health, aiming to address significant issues like anxiety, depression, and a lack of purpose in an increasingly complex society.

Eli believes in the power of literature to inspire, connect, and heal, aspiring to make his mark in the world through his work. He is a fresh and hopeful voice in literature and a source of support and motivation for those seeking a better understanding of themselves and the world around them. This writer is committed to advocating for a healthier and happier world!

Printed in Great Britain
by Amazon